HEALING
the
WOUND

HEALING
the
WOUND

Recovering from Loss

11-2010

RUTHANN FOX-HINES, PH.D.

To order additional copies of this book, contact:
Xlibris Corporation
1-888-795-4274
www.Xlibris.com
Orders@Xlibris.com
47741

CONTENTS

Dedication

In loving memory of Ruth Tomlinson Fox, John Paul Fox, Jeanie Brown Steele, Walter S. Brown Jr., Les Jones, and Evan (Eddie) Hines.

Chapter 1

Introduction

I am an expert on loss, partly because of my training as a counseling psychologist but mostly because of my personal history of losses. I lost my mother when I was twelve. I lost my sister when I was about twenty-five. I lost my father when I was in my late thirties. I lost my brother about ten years ago. Over the years, I have lost many friends to war, accidents, and disease. I never could *find* them—except through photo albums and memories and prayer—oh, and in the case of my father, via audiotapes. I lost my marriage near the time I lost my father. And since then, I have lost quite a few serious relationships. I lost my identity as a healthy woman via diagnosis with emphysema—no more hiking quickly up mountain trails. "Loss" is an interesting word. It's so gentle. It doesn't truly convey the pain, the fears, the depth of despair that often accompanies death, relationships ending, changes in life status.

With many years of my own therapy under my belt—often focused on the litany of losses—I became an expert in recovering from losses. I practiced on myself. I even drew up treatment plans and posted them on my refrigerator. Then I began to share this honed expertise with clients and with the broader community via workshops.

What I developed was practical. With many of my losses, I felt as if a great chunk of me had been ripped away and I had a bleeding open wound no one could really see but me. And that is when I began to think of healing from deaths and relationship disasters and discouraging life changes as similar to healing from a physical wound.

It is a model of self-care in the midst of crisis. Wounds need to be washed, anointed (every parent knows about Neosporin), bandaged. One often needs painkillers, medication. Most wounds call for stitches. And then there is the need for rehabilitation and, over time, attending to scar tissue.

Emotional wounds need the cleansing process of tears shed. They need soothing in terms of gentle kindnesses—often self-administered. Emotional wounds need the bandages of interpersonal support systems. Those that bare the wounds need the pain relief of distractions and the stitches of painful reality—he is dead, not passed on; the relationship is over; she is gone and with someone else; these legs will never run again. Plans for life after loss and setting those plans in place are aspects of rehabilitation. Noting painful anniversaries and honoring them are ways of consciously dealing with emotional scars.

The intent of this book is to provide guidance in drawing up a "treatment plan" for yourself as you move from the pain of the death of a loved one, the disruption of illness or injury, the loss of a dream or of the investment of self in a relationship through the healing process to reclaiming your life and your aliveness.

There will be worksheets and suggestions and examples with as little prescriptive advice as possible. Occasionally, when research strongly backs certain suggestions, they will be *strongly suggested.*

It may be of help to first realize that what you experience is most likely quite normal although it may feel *crazy.* Kübler-Ross in her book *On Death and Dying* outlined certain stages of grief—not as lockstep stages but as a guide for understanding the grief process. She identified the following five stages: denial, bargaining, depression, anger, and acceptance. Often it feels as if the stages are rolling over us like waves; sometimes we feel stuck in one of the stages. Applying the "treatment plan" can help you get unstuck—especially if you are stuck in the depression or anger stages.

"This isn't happening," "It can't be true," "She was just here yesterday," "My health is fine," "Our relationship is just hitting a bumpy place" are examples of the things we say to ourselves when we are in "denial."

Bargaining often includes pleas to God, "Dear God, don't let this be true," and making deals with the universe, "I'll be so understanding and patient and he will realize how wonderful I am and come back to me," "If she sees how much I am suffering, she will not leave me," "I'll do everything from now on that is healthy and the illness will go away."

Depression can extend from simple sadness and the blues through a full-scale clinical form of depression. Some symptoms—sleep problems, problems concentrating, not eating or overeating, not able to get much done—are normal and with application of the "treatment plan" can be moved past. Other symptoms including suicidal thoughts are more severe, and a therapist and possibly medication might be in order.

Anger can include anger with God for taking a loved one away, anger with the partner who left, displaced anger with the world because of an illness or injury. A danger with anger is that it feels more alive than depression and folks can get stuck in being angry because of the energy it provides. It is best to acknowledge the anger and find ways to channel its energy into productive activities: helping abused women in a shelter, getting victim protection laws passed, even digging a garden and planting vegetables for the homeless can be ways to redirect anger into productivity.

Acceptance is experienced as awareness of the realities of the absence of a loved one, the realities of the finality of a divorce, the realities of limitations incurred through illness or injury or loss of a job. It is expressed in making plans for the future and putting those plans in place.

It has been suggested that going through these stages is normal, and skipping stages or getting stuck in a stage can be harmful. If we look at this in terms of dealing with a wound:

Consider want happens to a wound that is ignored or neglected. It festers and becomes infected and can kill.

Consider what happens if we close a wound too soon, "I'm fine, thank you." Stiff upper lip. Again, infection and possible death.

What about overdoing painkillers? Addiction and debilitation. Throwing self into fourteen-hour workdays is not necessarily a healthy solution to an emotional wound. With overdoing medication, the wound is often closed too soon, infection grows, and eventually all the work in the world or all the play in the world cannot keep the infection from taking over the whole system.

How about picking at the scab or the stitches? This can be seen with people who leave everything in the home the way it was when the loved one died—the empty chair at the table, living with a ghost. This can be seen when people drive by the home of or call the former lover. Many of the unhealthy behaviors engaged in after a loss are either variations of overmedicating or of picking at the scab and causing reinfection. Many people, early in their grief, do scratch the scab; but eventually the wise ones use soothing ointments and bandages to keep themselves from picking, they do kindnesses for themselves, and they build and use their support system.

The remainder of this book will go into detail about each of the aspects of the "treatment plan": washing, applying ointment, bandaging, stitching, rehabilitating, and attending to scar tissue.

A warning: Please try not to turn the suggestions in this book into "shoulds." "Shoulds" cause an internal rebellion and sabotage the healing process. Try to focus on "wanting" to heal, wanting to allow the healing process to take place, wanting to assist with it via a personalized "treatment plan."

This idea of "shoulds" being negative comes out of a conceptualization of the personality as "top dog," "underdog," and "best friend"—sort of paralleling Freud's superego, id, and ego. Think of the voice in your head that says, "You should . . ." "I shouldn't . . ." "I have to . . ." "I must . . ." "A good person never . . ." That is the voice of the "top dog" (TD). We have a second dog, one that picks up on the messages of the TD and finds amazingly complex ways to sabotage the prescriptions of the TD. We then feel guilty, try harder, feel bad about ourselves, give up, etc. That opposing "dog" is the "underdog" (UD). Many of us lead our lives with a constant dogfight going on. We forget about the third aspect of our personhood, the "best friend" (BF). That part of us is deep within and is aware of what is good for us moment to moment; it is like a gyroscope. If we catch the dogfight going on, imagine pulling the dogs apart and then calling to that inner BF, who usually has whatever given name we truly cherish; the BF will let us know what we truly want. "I want to feel better about my body; therefore I will exercise" versus "I should exercise one hour every day, and I am a failure if I don't."

So as you read through the suggestions that follow, let your "best friend," that inner "wanting" not "shoulding" voice, be your guide. Tailor the suggestions to fit you—it is your "treatment plan."

Chapter 1 Exercises

Before continuing, it might be useful to stop and take stock of how you have dealt with losses in the past. What were you taught, what weren't you taught? What was allowed, what wasn't? *You may wish to get a notebook and designate it your "treatment plan" book, and begin by scribbling notes to yourself in response to the following questions:*

1. What were your earliest experiences with death, including the death of a pet?

2. What feeling do you recall having? With whom did you talk about your feeling? How were your feelings treated?

3. What were you told about death, its meaning, etc.?

4. What losses did you experience as a child: Moving or giving up friends? Loss of innocence via abuse? Injuries or illnesses that changed your lifestyle? Parents' divorce? Etc.?

5. How did the adult(s) in your life deal with these deaths or losses? How did they deal with you in regard to them?

6. How did your early experiences influence how you **feel** about death and/or loss now?

7. How do they relate to how you **deal** with death and/or loss now? Are you closer to the model suggested in this book or closer to inappropriate care—getting stuck in a stage or overdoing any one form of healing?

CHAPTER 2

WASHING THE WOUND

One of the first things we do when we have a cut is wash it; we try to cleanse it as best we can—clean water, soap, perhaps peroxide—and we do not simply clean it one time if it is a major wound. We cleanse it over and over; we irrigate it; we wash off as many sources of infection as possible.

Well, our emotional wounds call for the same type of cleansing; but in the case of emotional injuries, the cleansing agent is our tears. Yes, crying is healthy, and any of you who were taught "big boys or big girls don't cry" was done a major disservice. Tears are a form of release and symbolically allow some freedom from the pain of an emotional wound.

Our tears are more than simply a form of release. Tears cried for emotions are chemically different than tears cried while peeling an onion. The latter is mainly a saline wash while emotional tears actually contain chemicals related to negative affect and stress. When we cry for our losses, our hurt feelings, we are releasing harmful chemicals from our bodies. We are actually taking care of ourselves physically as well as emotionally.

I would also contend that tears cried with someone, witnessed tears, are better than tears cried alone. Crying alone is better than not crying, but crying with another adds connection to other humans to the benefits of shedding tears. In chapter 4, we will look more closely at the importance of connections with other people.

I suspect that in between crying alone and crying with someone who cares would be crying with a pet. Sometimes the closeness of a dog or a cat can provide a sense of being witnessed—especially a dog with its loving big eyes and warm, huggable body there to be held as we pour out some of our hurts. Even hugging a stuffed animal can be better than holding oneself as one cries.

If you are one of the unfortunate folks who learned not to cry, working on whatever blocks your freedom to cry when you are hurting emotionally would be a giant step toward healing. Consider the emotional infection you may be keeping within by withholding your tears.

If you are someone who cries easily but you are embarrassed about your tears, treasure them and see them as signs of the healing process at work. Stop apologizing for your tears, and help others learn about their value by letting them know the difference between onion tears and emotional tears.

If you are one of those people who learned to hide their hurt and sadness under a front of anger and usually find release in angry outbursts, consider how that drives others away and leaves you alone to deal with the pain deep within and consider the fact that you may be experiencing some form of release but not actually touching the pain that needs to be released. Our feelings are often like an onion with many levels; the surface may not be the "real" feeling. Frequently anger feels more alive than depression, so we move too quickly toward the anger when it is the deep sadness that needs attention. We push others away when what we truly need is to pull them close and feel the deeper feelings within the context of a connection with one who cares. At times anger may be part of healing, but that would come more as a form of handling stitches—realities of losses, which will be dealt with in chapter 6.

Remember our emotional wounds need to be washed as a way of cleaning out sources of infection just as our physical wounds need cleansing, and our tears are the major source of cleansing.

Chapter 2 Exercises

In order to understand yourself and your tears better, take some time and respond to the following questions:

1. What were you taught about crying?

   Did your father cry? If yes, how did that affect you? If no, what did that tell you about your own tears?

   Did your mother cry? If yes, how did that affect you? If no, what did that tell you about your own tears?

2. When can you cry?
   Circumstance?
   Events?
   Alone?
   With others?
   With a pet?

3. What might help you expand your crying repertoire?

4. Who, in your present life, can you cry with?

5. Who, in your present life, would it be very difficult to cry with? Why? Is there anything you could do to overcome that barrier?

6. Who in your present life, if you gave them a chance, might be a person with whom you could cry?
   What gets in the way of giving them a chance? What would it take to give them a chance?

If, after responding to these questions, you realize that you have great difficulty allowing yourself to cry and/or cry with someone else, it could help to find a therapist who would assist you in exploring at more depth the blocks you have to allowing tears as a release and/or the block you have toward allowing yourself to be consoled by others.

CHAPTER 3

OINTMENT

Those of you that are parents are probably very familiar with the wonders of Neosporin—or similar ointments—for our children's injuries. And I bet the vast majority of us in our childhood experienced our parents' use of infection-preventing salves. With emotional injuries, healing, infection-preventing ointment is also needed, yet many of us were not trained to care for emotional wounds as cautiously and diligently as we were taught to take care of physical ones, yet it is just as necessary.

In the realm of the emotional pain that accompanies loss, whether the death of a loved one, the death of a relationship, or the death of a dream, "ointments" that heal feelings and prevent emotional infections—festering anger, debilitating sorrow—are needed. Emotional "ointments" come in many forms, and in this chapter, I want to suggest a wide variety of them. They usually come in one of two major categories: self-care and acceptance of care. Some forms of both are essential for deep healing of emotional injuries, and self-care includes attending to both emotional and physical well-being.

Emotional injuries often affect the appetite causing either a loss of the desire to eat or a drive to devour whatever is in sight—especially if it's "bad." Being aware of this possibility and attending to nutrition is important. Enlisting family or friends in this may be important. (I recall during one of my times of grief, totally forgetting to eat or looking in the fridge and seeing nothing I wanted, dear friends would call and ask, "Have you eaten today?" "Well, I had some yogurt." "OK, I'm coming over in half an hour and we're going to lunch—no arguments!" With future losses, I would put reminders on the refrigerator about eating even if nothing tasted good.) Taking vitamin supplements might also be a good addition to your routine or if it is already part of your routine, making sure not to neglect it.

Overeating when in grief may be a form of self-nurturing, an unhealthy form, and trying some of the suggestions in this chapter and in chapter 4 instead may help. Sometimes overeating—foraging, biting, chewing—may be a release for the angry feelings that usually accompany loss, especially if there are family or cultural restrictions on acknowledging one is angry or expressing anger. Again, some of the suggestions in this chapter and in chapter 5 may be useful.

Attending to physical appearance is also a form of "ointment." Bathing, grooming, dressing in clean clothing, etc., can help build the sense of your life, your aliveness, your being alive in the world despite loss. Getting a massage, getting a pedicure, or any other physical pampering can be healing and can be reminders that you are important and that there are pleasures in life despite loss. Take a bubble bath, light candles, wrap yourself in something soothing—silk, your granny's quilt, an old flannel shirt, whatever. Get your old stuffed animal out of storage and cuddle it.

Open the shades, let light into your home. Light is essential to emotional well-being. There is a form of depression, SAD (seasonal affective disorder), that is "cured" by exposure to full-spectrum light. All humans need light, yet when we are hurting, we often hide in the dark. Yes, people in the midst of suffering from such disorders as migraine headaches may have problems with light, but aside from that, light reminds us of life, and full-spectrum light (i.e., sunshine or light provided by special lamps) does affect our emotional well-being; it can raise our spirits.

Sleep is another area that often is affected when grieving—too much or too little. If you find yourself sleeping more than is normally healthy for you, at first you may need that escape; if it continues for weeks, it becomes an unhealthy escape. Try enticing yourself to get up by using whatever might serve as a healthy reward for you. It may just be to head straight to the shower and allow the water to flow over you until you've used all the hot water. If you find you are sleeping significantly less than your normal amount, at first don't fight it—use the time to journal, to cry, to cuddle with a pet. If the insomnia persists, begin implementing the various strategies for sleeping: avoiding caffeine in late afternoon and evening, avoiding exercise in the evening, establishing or reestablishing a bedtime routine that signals time to sleep—for some folks it's prayer, for some it's a couple of pages of a boring book. If you wake up and can't sleep, return to journaling, shedding the accumulated tears, soothing with music—again, whatever works. (A friend suggested that if I couldn't sleep, I get up and do the chores I hate the most—cleaning toilets, ironing. I soon found that my body began to cooperate with choosing to sleep over the chores.)

Get out of the house—even if it is to sit on the porch or stoop and experience that there is a world out there to be experienced despite the fact that some of the world you've known has been shattered. See the roses, see the hardy flowering weeds that push through the cement. Moving—going outdoors and walking around the block, maybe extend that to a few blocks—can help the body produce mood-elevating chemicals and can serve as a reminder that we are still functioning human beings.

Meditation, yoga, self-hypnosis can be marvelous forms of physical and mental self-care. *The Relaxation Response* (2000, original publication 1975) is one of the earliest and best books on healing relaxation. Check your bookstore for books, DVDs, cassettes, and CDs with instructions and aids for this form of self-care.

Prayer is also a wonderful form of healing for those who consider themselves spiritual and/or religious. Especially for the prayerful person, talking with whatever one's image of God is can be soothing and reaffirming of life. Sitting in silence and allowing that Being(s) to "talk" to us can be healing and affirming. Reading inspirational literature and attending services more frequently than usual can also be of help in difficult times.

Engaging in the rituals of one's faith can be emotionally healing. Funeral and memorial services are usually helpful, although they often occur when one is still in a "numb," one-foot-in-front-of-the-other reaction. Later it is often helpful to create rituals specific to our own losses. There are books available in the public library that can be of assistance in this. However, simple rituals of assembling a photo display of a dead loved one; reading and then putting away in a special place letters from a lost love; or, if the lost love is one who abandoned you, burning the letters or gathering presents and donating them to charity might be appropriate rituals.

Just as physical wounds often need the infection drained out, clearing out the infection of emotional wounds is usually necessary. Externalizing feelings versus keeping them hidden away inside can be very healing. When we are in the throes of grief, the hurt, the sadness, the anger, the possible guilt or pitiful sense of self need to be extracted and not left to fester and/or to find their own ways out—often inappropriately, e.g., angry outbursts with minor infractions by innocent people.

There are many approaches to this form of self-care including writing. When journaling, I recommend a simple notebook, at least in the beginning, because attractive journals often cause us to feel we have to write attractive thoughts, and the feelings and thoughts we have when we are grieving are often not that attractive. You might want to have an attractive journal in which you assemble positive memories and celebrate the person, the relationship, the way of life that is now gone; but I believe there does need to be some place to unload the unacceptable feelings and thoughts. For people with a creative bent, writing poetry or fictionalized versions of one's stories may be a helpful approach. (I once wrote several haiku honoring a budding romance. When the relationship died, part of my healing was writing several pages of haiku about the disintegration of the romance.)

Another form of externalizing can be drawing, painting, or other creative expressions, the goal of which is not a work of art but a creation that may celebrate a life or just the opposite, it may express feelings of anger and frustration that one cannot express verbally.

At the beginning of this chapter, I mentioned that in addition to self-care, there was acceptance of care from others. In the next chapter, we will look at the importance of other people in the healing process. For now, I simply want to say that sharing the writing or the art with understanding and accepting others can add to the positive effects of the activity. Here, it is important to mention that talking with a truly good friend or working with a therapist to disinfect the wound can be a major source of self-care, of healing. Seeking and accepting the listening, the shoulder, the kindnesses of friends and seeking and accepting the care of a counselor, a therapist, or a pastor are all ways to allow the process of healing to take place.

With physical wounds, it doesn't help to pretend infection isn't present and that it doesn't need clearing out and infection prevention. Our emotional wounds are the same. There is a need for "ointment" or more realistically several forms of ointment and many, many applications. All of those mentioned in this chapter most likely will not apply, but some of them should, and utilizing one or more from each of the inferred categories—physical and emotional; self-care in the form of nutrition, light, exercise, etc.; self-care in the form of mental/emotional activities; self-help in the form of externalizing negative feelings; and help in the form of seeking and accepting help—can blend into an effective "ointment" for the wound you have suffered.

Chapter 3 Exercises

1. Create a personalized "ointment" plan—starting with this outline:

By each of the headings below, try to write what you are doing that relates to that heading and what you will do as part of your healing. Try to have something for most categories, but do not beat up on yourself about blanks—focus your energy on applying the "ointment" you have identified.

PHYSICAL SELF-CARE	EMOTIONAL SELF-CARE
Nutrition	Meditation/Self-Hypnosis/Yoga
Physical Appearance	Prayer Spiritual/Religious Reading Spiritual/Religious Activities
Physical Pampering	Rituals: 　Faith Based 　Own Creation 　Ideas from Books
Light	Journaling Creative Writing Creative Activities
Getting Outdoors/Movement	Counseling/Therapy *(see exercise 2)*
Other	Other

Exercise 1 continued.

> After filling in the overall "ointment" plan, ask friends for. suggestions that you might add to the list.

> When the "ointment" plan is complete (for now, you can always add things as you think of them or get ideas from reading, from talking with others, etc.), post the plan where you can refer to it easily.

> Make daily and/or weekly contracts to engage in the things you've listed. You might even get a pad of paper and label each page, "Ointment Plan for Today or for Week (Date)."

> When making contracts, be sure to be kind and gentle with yourself—and realistic. Avoid "every day," "always," and other potentially punishing words or phrases. Use the more realistic term "at least": "I will ＿＿ at least ＿＿ time(s) this week." Then, if you do it more, you can feel super special, but you will have met your goal and not failed if you accomplish whatever you identified as "at least," and make sure you start out with very easy "at leasts."

2. Ask a friend, colleague, relative, clergy member, or physician for recommendations regarding counseling/therapy and/or support groups available in the community either privately or through various agencies. Often hospitals have counseling options and support groups available for people that are grieving whether it be because of death of a person or the death of a lifestyle brought on by illness or an accident.

> If possible get at least three suggestions and call up the provider and interview each to get a sense of right fit for you (gender, training, approach, fees, etc.) Make an appointment and try to commit to at least three sessions; usually one session is not enough to get what you need, even what you need in terms of finding out if the person or group is what you are hoping for.

Chapter 4

Bandage

I think we all know the importance of bandaging a major wound, but little cuts may especially need the protection of a Band-Aid because although it appears to be only a little cut, it can be the entrance for great infection. So it is with our emotional wounds. The big wounds such as death of a loved one need the protection of bandages for sure, but the "little" ones—end of a bad relationship, a miscarriage, an illness that takes away the ability to do certain things, not getting a promotion, being robbed, etc.—only appear minor to the outside world; inside, we often know how bad they hurt and how easily they may become infected by feelings of guilt and frustration and hopelessness.

In the case of emotional wounds, the bandage is our interpersonal support system—the people in our lives whom we trust to care for us, be there for us, accept us, guide us, even gently and empathically challenge us. Just as bandages are used to keep physical wounds safe, we need the psychological protection of the attention and support from caring people.

Please note the term is "support system," which indicates more than one person. One fellow human being, no matter how much that person may love us, cannot be a "system." One is better than none; but any single human being eventually will let us down, will fail to be all we need—not because he or she does not love us, or care about us, but simply because she or he is human and can never be everything for him- or herself, let alone for another human being.

Humans need other humans. Much research supports the fact that isolation is debilitating and can exacerbate illnesses, etc. Personality differences such as those described in the literature on the Myers-Briggs Type Indicator (MBTI), a personality inventory that measures preferences for how to be in the world, point to differences in the numbers of connections with others but does not support the idea of no connections. According to the MBTI, some people have a strong need for many interpersonal connections, and that preference is referred to as "extroverted" preference; other people prefer to have connections with only a few others, and that preference is referred to as "introverted" preference. The main idea here, though, is that whether it is many or a few, some other humans are needed in our lives—especially when we are trying to recover from an emotional wound.

It is important to understand that simply by being in our lives all people—relatives, friends, colleagues, etc.—are not immediately useful as part of a support system. Some in fact may contribute to the possibilities for infection. The people who say, "You're doing so well," often mean "I sure hope you're doing well 'cause I don't want to have to do anything." Not always, but too often. Relatives and friends may have their own agendas hidden in the advice they give. Some folks may simply not have it in them to be supportive or may be too stressed out to have anything to give in the moment. So it is important to be selective in choosing who makes up your support system, but remember, it is a system, and make sure to select several people to comprise your bandage or bandages.

Pines and Aronson, in their book *Burnout* (1981), suggested that there are several forms of interpersonal support people need. Three of the categories they delineated are of significant importance here: emotional support, emotional challenge, and social validation.

The first is **emotional support.** People who fit this category are capable of accepting you as you are, simply being there, and affirming your right to your feelings—all of them, nice feelings and not-so-nice feelings such as depression, anger, or frustration. They do not tell you to feel something you are not feeling. "Cheer up; it's for the best" is not what comes out of the mouths of people who are able to provide emotional support. (When my father was dying in the hospital, I had many frustrating encounters with his physician. After one such encounter, which I handled assertively in front of the MD and his bevy of residents, I retreated to my father's room; and the priest who'd been seeing me through much of the decisions, etc., showed up. I burst into tears and began cussing up a storm. He simply took me in his arms and let me sob. Never a word about my cussing, etc. No corrections. No admonishments. Simple and wonderful support.)

The second is **emotional challenge.** The need to heal includes assistance in gaining different, even new, perspectives. It is important to have one or two people who can provide emotional support and who have the skill, talent, ability to nudge you beyond where you are.

They ask the right questions; they offer a different view—not negating your existing one but providing a different way of looking at things. They can help us go beyond the immediate feelings and move toward understanding, acceptance, and perhaps even change.

Usually this kind of support is best found in counseling and therapy with professionals trained to provide emotional support and then build on it with challenges that fit and help us move toward greater healing. Sometimes we are blessed with a special friend or even a relative who has the innate ability to provide this form of support, but most of the time, it is necessary to seek it in a professional setting as suggested in chapter 3.

The third form of support delineated by Pines and Aronson is **social validation.** This consists of people who, in different areas of our lives, hold values similar to ours and who have had similar experiences. These people help us realize we are not "crazy"; these are people who help us feel we are not alone or feel as if we were reindeer at the equator.

People going through divorce often need to talk with others going through a divorce, but even then there may be a need to sort out those who not only have similar experiences but also have similar values, e.g., when there is a divorce because the marriage died not because either party was a bitch or bastard, there may be a need for others who have the sadness of that death. People who have been through angry and mean litigation may not be very helpful; in fact, they could be harmful.

People who had a difficult relationship with a relative who just died may not get validation from those who were close and experienced that person differently. They may need to find others who experience relief or absence of sorry that a significant figure is dead.

Frequently issues of faith and religious and/or spiritual beliefs arise during times of loss—deaths, endings of relationships, debilitating illnesses, etc. We need people whose beliefs are similar to ours, not people who impose their values and beliefs in the name of being helpful, e.g., when suffering the dismantlement of a marriage, one doesn't need guilt trips about trying harder or who's to blame. Most people who reach the point of divorce have tried very hard, and the grieving person needs to avoid those who would add to the pain by questioning and judging.

It is important to be alert in regard to those who fit in this category and those who do not. It is important to give credence and be open to the ones who fit and to protect oneself from those who do not—at times, perhaps, avoiding those persons for at least a while. Past behavior is often the best predictor of future behavior, so if one experiences an individual offering support that is not helpful and may even feel as if it is coming out of some personal agenda—he or she may want to convert one to a religious belief, the individual may want to "fix" rather than support—it is important to note that and not look to that person in the future.

I would add a fourth form of support: **practical support**. One that is often very much needed at the beginning of dealing with losses, and that is the support given by people who mainly know how to show care and concern by taking action, by doing, by attending to the many practical needs that arise at times of crisis and loss.

These beautiful souls are the ones who clean up the house, bring food, take care of pets and plants, help with arrangements for funerals and/or for legal action, take care of transportation needs, sometimes provide monetary assistance. They give what they can, and thank goodness for what they give. They may be the "Marthas," but what Martha provided to Jesus and his friends in the New Testament was necessary. Doing is their form of loving and caring.

It is important to include them in your support system, to allow them to care and provide for your practical needs. This is not the time for "I can do it all myself." There is usually enough pain to cope with without adding unnecessary stress by trying to take care of everything yourself. Some of the people who fit in this category may need to know what would be helpful and welcome your telling them that you need someone to pick up the cleaning, accompany you to an appointment, take care of a pet, etc.

Occasionally you may be truly blessed by finding a few people who are capable of providing more than one of the forms of support. Be thankful, but be careful not to slip into looking to them for everything. Remember it is a **support system**; and although those beautiful human beings provide much of the care we need, they are human, they are imperfect creatures, and they cannot be all or do all. In general I'd suggest that we have at least four or five folks in the first category, one or two in the second, many in the third, and several in the fourth.

One source of possibly finding several of the forms of support is in formally established support groups, whether it be bereavement groups, divorce survivor groups, twelve-step groups, or groups for people facing specific diseases or disabilities. Religious organizations, hospitals, and mental health centers are major providers of such services. Often these are listed in sections of newspapers or can be found by calling the organizations mentioned above. It may take awhile to find the right fit, but as I suggested in chapter 3, try to attend a given group three times before deciding it isn't the right one for you.

Questions arise about the usefulness of chat rooms as sources of support. Research is limited. Some cyberspace interactions may be good—especially if they connect you with a source of social validation, with others who understand your loss. In the long run, though, cyberspace is not our real, walking-around life space (anyone can pretend to be anything out there in cyberspace); and we need to build real human contact as a major form of our bandage, of our support system.

Remember, in times of emotional pain, we need the bandage of human support. There may be times when it is healthy to temporarily expose a wound to the air without a bandage, and there may be times to not have the emotional bandage of a support system, time for solitude and space from others. It's a matter of balance: time for solitary activities such as prayer or meditation and time to be with truly supportive others.

Chapter 4 Exercises

1. Using the chart below, fill in names (with phone numbers if possible) of people in your life who fit in the categories.

CATEGORIES	DEFINITELY FIT	PROBABLY FIT	POSSIBLY FIT
Emotional Support			
Emotional Challenge			
Social Validation			
Practical Support			

2. Consider if there are blanks in column 1 or only a minimal number of names. What would you need to do to move names from columns 2 and 3? Make a few calls and tell those folks you're not in a good place and need some support? Ask for something specific? What's the worst that can happen—they say no or offer help you don't want and you learn that they don't fit in either column 1 or 2 or that they may only be able to fit in a category different from the one in which you had them listed?

3. Make a contract to contact/connect with at least one of the people in column 1—especially in the first, third, and fourth categories—at least once a day (no less than a few times a week). Write the contract down and keep it where you will remember to carry through.

4. Especially if you have only a few names in column 1, make a contract to contact/connect with people from the other two columns and investigate if they can be moved to column 1 or to another category.

5. If you find yourself with an almost-blank list and lack the energy to investigate other possibilities, at least contract to locate a support group and/or a counselor/therapist.

6. Even if you have a good support system—i.e., your categories and columns, especially column 1, are adequately filled with different names—seeking professional help in the form of a counselor or therapist and/or joining a support group could help the healing process move along. If you do have a therapist/counselor, make sure to see him or her regularly.

CHAPTER 5
MEDICATION/PAINKILLERS

Pain medication is frequently prescribed when we suffer major wounds, and our emotional wounds often call for help with managing the pain that accompanies them. Sometimes the medication for emotional wounds is actually medication in the form of sleep aids, anxiety-preventing drugs, and perhaps antidepressants; but those can be overdone. Some people attempt to medicate their emotional pain via alcohol or even illegal drugs—zoning out on pot, passing out on whiskey—and these forms of medicating can be very debilitating.

The medication or painkillers we are looking at in this chapter come in the forms of distractions and/or activity. These include all of the activities that often accompany a loss—with deaths, making funeral, burial, and cremation arrangements, dealing with legal matters, informing relatives, etc.; with relationship endings, there can be legal matters, informing people, taking care of such practicalities as relocation, reestablishing a home; with major life changes, the practicalities can absorb a lot of energy. I refer to these activities as "taking care of business." These are activities that can take much of our time, thought, and energy as we are immersed in the practical chores and details that need to be taken care of. They often provide us with a sense of control during a period when we feel helpless—at least we're doing something.

It is healthy to engage in this form of medicinal activity. It remains unhealthy to overuse any form of painkillers or to rely only on medication and not engage in washing and rewashing, not continue to apply healing ointment, or not to maintain clean bandaging.

Returning to work, resuming home chores, or getting back into daily life activities is another form of activity that can serve to dull emotional pain. It is important to be kind and gentle with oneself when doing this: keep the standards relatively low, **do not make major decisions**, do not take on extra work or extra challenges until the healing process is well along. Some people turn into workaholics in their overuse of work as a means of dealing with the pains of loss. Moderation, gentleness, and remembering to attend to the wound—not ignore it—are the cautions connected with looking to work as an aspect of dealing with emotional wounds.

Physical self-care was mentioned in chapter 3. Here again its usefulness needs to be noted. Planning healthy meals and attending to appearance can be very healthy distractions.

Exercise is extraordinarily helpful when it comes to coping with emotional pain: when we exercise, our bodies produce chemicals that are related to elevated mood. Getting out and walking is a wonderful activity with little getting in the way of actually doing it, unless one is physically disabled.

Engaging in sports activities—tennis, softball, soccer, etc.—can not only help in the form of producing positive chemicals but can also be part of the bandage, i.e., interactions with other human beings. The same goes for joining yoga, aerobics, karate, or other physically involved classes that provide physical, mental, and, often, interactive activity.

The caution once again is to use these with moderation: moderation in the challenges one sets for oneself, moderation in the amount of time and energy invested, moderation in the form of not neglecting the other aspects of caring for the wound.

Another form of medication that is important to include in your emotional medicine chest is whatever you experience as lightness—play, laughter, whatever was or can be fun for you. TV, movies, music, reading, computer games, surfing the Net, and creative activities constitute a form of distractions that is useful but can be dangerous in the solitary nature of those activities. Too much solitary activity may result in neglect of the bandage—developing and maintaining a support system. Try to find folks who enjoy the same movies or DVDs and invite them over. Join a book club. Do not allow the medications/distractions you employ to keep you isolated.

Playing games, finding people and things that make you laugh, getting out socially, accepting invitations to go out and play, entertaining, shopping with a friend, and participating in fun classes are all wonderful and necessary distractions—if not overdone.

If you have difficulty thinking of what might be fun for you, consider what was fun for you when you were a child. Often childhood play can be joyful play for grown-ups. Fly a kite. Ride a bike. Visit an amusement park and ride the rides and eat cotton candy. (I celebrate my mother's life by having tea parties using her fine china teacups—pinky out of course, sometimes dressing up and inviting special women friends to join me.)

Laughter is especially healing. It, like exercise, helps the body create positive chemicals that serve to raise our spirits. Even fake laughing can turn into real and be of benefit.

Getting involved in politics or in civic or religious organizations' activities can be useful distractions. Volunteering and doing altruistic service can be very healing—taking the energy of anger and using it for good can be especially healing. The usual caution exists: do not turn these into a source of stress and debilitation by over investing and overdoing. Keep the purpose in mind, and that purpose is to help with the healing process. As you heal, you may find that you want these things as part of your new life; but during healing, especially the earlier phases, keep the awareness of the need for all the other aspects of healing.

Distractions and activities as medication are an important part of the healing process. Having a "medicine chest" with a variety of possibilities is important. Sometimes one medication works; sometimes it doesn't. Taking care of business can raise all sorts of memories that may need to be journaled about or talked about with a counselor before it can return to being emotionally useful. Physical activities, sports, games, etc., can lose their usefulness if they become too competitive and stressful. Laughter often finds itself paired with tears by bringing memories of laughing with a lost loved one or lover. Welcome both because they both contribute to healing.

This isn't the time to turn into an alcoholic, a workaholic, or even a playaholic, but it is not healthy to spend the majority of your time focused on the loss, so diversions in the form of work and play, etc., are appropriate. It is a very valid quest to seek relief from pain. What we choose to use to relieve the pain can be healing or harmful. How we use our painkillers can be healing or harmful. Variety and moderation and mixing the use of emotional medications with our emotional support systems are key to proper use.

Chapter 5 Exercises

1. Fill in information under the following headings:

ACTIVITIES THAT ARE FUN FOR ME, OF INTEREST TO ME	ALONE (check)	WITH OTHERS (check)	NAMES AND PHONE NUMBERS (if possible) OF PEOPLE WITH WHOM I MIGHT BE ABLE TO SHARE THIS ACTIVITY

2. Ask friends or relatives for suggestions to add to the list.

3. As suggested in the chapter, think back to childhood. Are there any games or activities you could add to your list from that part of your life?

4. Make a daily contract to do at least one small fun thing a day—go out to lunch with a friend, take a bubble bath, play racquetball with a colleague, go to a movie, watch a favorite TV show without trying to do three chores at the same time.

5. Make a weekly contract to engage in larger diversion projects. Have a dinner party for a couple of friends, read a book, repaint a room, make a holiday shopping list and begin catalogue shopping.

6. Make a list of things you need to do in terms of dealing with the particulars of the loss. Write thank-you notes, deal with a will, make therapy appointments and keep the appointments, etc. Ask friends and/or experts (attorneys, therapists, physicians, clergy members.) for help with the list.

7. Make daily contracts to do something from the list each day—even if it is only to look up a phone number of a person or agency to call the next day.

CHAPTER 6

STITCHES

Physical healing generally includes some pain, often in the form of stitches. The necessary pain related to emotional healing is accepting our angry feelings and facing the pain of **reality.**

For some people, the angry feelings come easily—too easily. People can get stuck in that stage of the healing process. Anger feels better than depression. There is some energy related to anger. We can point fingers and feel temporary relief. The relief doesn't last if the range of feelings isn't dealt with. The anger can feed on itself and create a cycle of emotional explosions, angry distancing, exaggerated blaming, searching for enemies, and other toxic behaviors—toxic to self and frequently to others.

Acknowledging anger is important. Deciding what we do with it is very important. Rather than allowing it to gush out in tirades or behaviors we later regret, it is a good thing to find healthy ways of expressing it, even using the energy that it provides to take action, channeled action, action for a cause, action to get things done. It is often helpful to have a therapist you can bring your anger to and from whom you can get assistance in expressing it and clearing it away in nondestructive, possibly even constructive, ways.

Some people are so afraid of their anger that they stuff it inside, hide it, ignore it, pretend it isn't there, deny its existence. Many people have been taught that anger is bad, evil, a sin, not ladylike. Unfortunately simply denying its existence does not alter its existence. It's there, and it will find some form of expression. For some, it slips out in angry outbursts; for others, it oozes out in passive-aggressive behavior (e.g., "I'm a kind and good person and I would never hurt anyone," but the behaviors—cutting remarks, negative facial expressions, especially behind another's back, forgetting things important to others—seep out.)

Sometimes we are afraid to direct our anger where it belongs so we direct it toward someone or something that feels safer—we may be angry because of the loss of a job, but we take it out on our spouses; we may be angry because we've been diagnosed with a debilitating disease, but we take it out on the physician who provided the diagnosis; we may be angry with God for allowing something bad to happen, but we take it out on "the system."

Sometimes it sits so deep inside, it festers and eats at us, and our negative feelings about ourselves intensify, and we experience internal agony. One of the classic definitions of depression is anger turned inward.

A formula for dealing with difficult feeling such as anger is one I created and have taught for many years titled "Four Steps in Dealing with Feelings."

Four Steps in Dealing with Feelings

1. Acceptance: Accept that you are human, and humans have feelings and emotions **as well as** thoughts and ideas. The feeling aspect is not bad, unworthy, unimportant. It is part of what makes you fully human, and it is as worthy and important as the thinking, rational aspect of self. You are capable of the whole gamut of feelings from those you've been taught are OK, good, nice, acceptable through those you've been taught are not OK, bad, unacceptable, dangerous. Love, caring, sympathy, and patience are some of the feelings usually weighted as "good." Fear, anger, hurt, and jealousy usually are weighted as "bad." Humans have ALL those feelings. Acknowledging them when experienced is healthier

than shoving them deeper inside by ignoring them, pretending not to have them, fooling oneself into believing one is "above" experiencing the "negative" feelings. It is better to acknowledge feelings—especially the ones we "shouldn't" have or the ones that we have learned may be "dangerous": "I'm feeling _____, and that is OK because it is human to feel. Now, what do I want to do with this feeling?"

2. Nondestructive Expression: Once you have acknowledged you feel a certain feeling or combination of feelings, it is important to find some way to express those feelings in a way that is safe and not harmful to ourselves or to others. This applies to the "good" feelings as well as the "bad" feelings. Some people overdo such things as expressing love and caring and end up smothering others. With the "bad" feelings, this step is sometimes referred to as catharsis or ventilation—similar to throwing up when one has food poisoning. Examples of useful ways to ventilate include running, beating a pillow, using a punching bag, screaming into a towel, crying into a pillow or crying with a friend, kneading bread, scrubbing floors, and throwing darts at a dartboard. Two nonphysical ways of getting feelings out are (a) write feelings, circumstances, thoughts out on paper—perhaps as a letter never mailed and later destroyed, and (b) talk about feelings, etc., with a friend or counselor who doesn't judge the feelings we expose to them.

3. Redirection: This is now the time to begin to use the thinking functions. After expression of feelings, it is often good to stop and take several nice, deep slow breaths. This sort of breathing is calming. As relaxation increases, ask yourself, "What do I want to do about this?" "Are there any actions that would be helpful to take?" "What would be the most helpful, useful thing to do now?"

4. Action: This is the rational step: consider the facts, the situation, the consequences, etc. This is where things are put into perspective and decisions made: decisions to act (make an assertive request, lodge an assertive complaint, leave a relationship, etc.) or to not

act (truly let go of the feeling, decide that "in the great cosmic picture" it isn't worth your energy.)

So dealing with the angry feelings, experiencing them, and sorting them out is a task of healing. Usually an unpleasant task—as stitches are with wounds—but a necessary one. Some of the suggestions in chapter 3 such as journaling and/or seeing a therapist can help with this.

The other very difficult task of healing is facing the realities of the loss. It can be very painful at first to use such phrases as "He is dead," "The relationship is over," "My legs are gone," "I need to take medication possibly the rest of my life." These real words are part of moving on to acceptance and rehabilitation (chapter 7)—emotional and sometimes physical.

Our culture doesn't help a lot with this part of healing. Euphemisms are the dominant way of referring to painful happenings. Friends, relatives, and even clergy often resort to these—"She's **passed**," "It's **for the best**," "You'll find a better relationship **soon**," "You are strong and I know you will be OK." All are "nice" ways of circumventing the facts and avoiding reality: "Someone I loved has **died** and I won't see them again (at least in this life)"; "Even though the marriage wasn't that good, I had dreams and hopes, and those hopes and dreams are now **dead** with the divorce"; "Even though I survived, my legs are **gone**, and my world is drastically different."

Many people do not want to think about their own mortality, the previous deaths of loved ones, the approaching deaths of older beloved relatives, the possibility of themselves having to face the debilitation of a major illness or injury, or the possibility of their own relationships ending; so they have a difficult time being with you in facing your realities.

This is why it is so important to value those friends who can be with you in the painful reality of reality, to wrap those people around you as a major part of your bandage, your support system. Sometimes we do not have people who can do this. Then it is especially important to find a counselor or therapist who is trained to be with people in pain, trained to help people face sometimes agonizing realities.

We can do some of the reality work on our own—note "some," not all—via journaling, via creative expressions, via beginning to use the real words. Others may be "shocked," but that is their issue, and your self-care is the primary concern when you are healing.

Reality is the basis for acceptance, and acceptance is the basis for rehabilitation. Reality can be harsh, and it should rarely be faced alone. Avoiding it leaves you stuck, looking backward, resisting the steps for moving on, and not living the one life you have major control of—your life.

Chapter 6 Exercises

1. If you have been journaling as suggested in chapter 3, continue, but make sure to now use the "real" words (dead, finished, etc.) if you haven't been doing that already.

2. What were you taught about anger? What were your role models? As objectively as possible, do you consider what you were taught healthy? If not, who in your life space might serve as a good role model?

3. Do you freely express anger? Would you say you get stuck in anger? Or do you swallow your anger? If you swallow it, where does it go?

4. If, in answering question #3, you found that you either have angry outbursts or get stuck in anger or you swallow it and perhaps experience it as depression, getting into therapy might be a very important step.

5. Try applying the "Four Steps in Dealing with Feelings" at least one time this week, and then work up to as often as at least once a day.

    A. Identify a feeling you are having, especially one considered "bad," and have a little talk with yourself in your head about being human and accepting the fact that you can have all feelings—"good" ones and "bad" ones.

    B. Find some nonharmful expression for that feeling (see the steps for suggestions) and employ it.

    C. Stop, breathe, and ask yourself the questions suggested in the steps.

    D. Decide if you wish to take action, truly let the feeling go, put it on the back burner for work later.

    E. You may wish to keep a notebook where you record your efforts in regard to this. If you find it isn't working, talk it over with your therapist, or now may be the time to start seeing a counselor.

9. Look over your support systems list. Are there any people on that list who could serve as outlets for your not-so-nice feelings without inadvertently "helping" you get stuck in the negative feeling? Are there any people on the list who can be there as you deal with the realities without euphemisms, etc.? Write their names below, and make minicontracts to connect with them soon. If there are not individuals who can provide this type of support, all the more reason to seek counseling/therapy at this point.

CHAPTER 7

REHABILITATION

As you work through the first aspects of healing—the washing, the ointment, the bandaging, the medication, and the stitches—you move closer and closer to the "acceptance" stage of grieving. Remember, stages are not lockstep; rather we often roll through them in waves. Attending to the wound, especially the stitches (chapter 6) where we face and begin to accept the reality of the loss, sets the stage for rehabilitation, for beginning to plan for life after a wound, for beginning to get on with our own lives—perhaps in much altered ways, but to get on with the tasks and potential joys of simply being alive.

If the loss is the death of a loved one, the rehabilitation will call for figuring out how to honor the life of the person you loved without losing your life in the process. It will mean looking into ways of experiencing the good things we experienced with that loved one without trying to replace the loved one, e.g., getting some maternal love from an older aunt versus getting another mother, experiencing the joy of cuddling a baby by helping in a nursery for babies born with AIDS versus rushing on to another pregnancy too quickly, learning how to manage money ourselves if the dead loved one or the divorced partner was the breadwinner and manager versus ending up in giant credit card debt, learning to cook and clean versus living in a dirty "bachelor pad."

Rehabilitation often calls for learning skills we once were able to do or relied on others (usually the person who is gone) to provide. This may call for attending classes to learn those skills. This may call for joining specific support groups where participants encourage each other as they learn to do the things others once did. Continuing education classes in local community colleges and classes and groups provided by community agencies, hospitals, and churches can be very helpful in this aspect of getting back into your life.

With the death of a loved one who has suffered over a long period and/or with the death of a loved one who needed much of your care and energy over a long period, one of the feelings we often have is a sense of relief, and yet we may feel guilty for feeling that. Allowing yourself that feeling as well as all the other possible feelings is important. It's true that there are folks who might look askance at such a nongrieving feeling, but people who fit in the first category of a support system (chapter 4) are people who will fully understand and accept you and all your feelings. Accept the freedom that the relief may bring as energy to move into your own intensive rehabilitation.

Similar to what is needed with the death of a loved one, a wound resulting from the death of a relationship calls for rehabilitation in the form of activities that assert your wholeness as a person and your value as an individual. Many of the activities suggested in chapters 3, 4, and 5 should help with this.

With a broken relationship, the reality work, the stitches, is necessary before moving on into another relationship. If you rush on into another relationship, you bring all the unfinished business of the first. If that is a pattern through several relationships, you may be carrying around a lot of unfinished business. Rehabilitation calls for assessing the lessons learned from the dead relationship(s)—not in sarcastic forms of "Well, I learned never to trust a man (or woman) again" but more in the sense of learning you are attracted to exciting but untrustworthy men (or women) and that perhaps you might give ordinary, "boring" men (or women) a chance in the future. Talking with a therapist/counselor can be especially helpful with this part of rehabilitation. Finishing up the business of the dead relationship is the best starting point for a new relationship. The best step is often *moving on with your life,* validating who you are as an individual, before *moving into another relationship.*

Rehabilitation may call for a change of scenery not to escape sadness but to assert your individuality, your personhood, despite the death of a loved one or the end of a significant relationship. It may call for changing the scenery within the home—not leaving an empty chair at the table, not leaving everything as it was before our loved one died. Redecorating—not necessarily a total makeover—may be therapeutic and mix rehab with the medication of activities in a project. It may possibly call for actually moving. For instance, if the space shared was so small, there is no room to reclaim the space as yours or if the space was so large, and perhaps expensive, that you cannot maintain it on your own. Finding a space that fits for you may again be both rehab and medication in the form of a project.

When the loss is a major change in lifestyle due to physical causes—permanent injuries with major debilitations (loss of sight, mobility, athletic prowess, etc.), diagnosis with illnesses that are potentially limiting (e.g., emphysema, MS, and cancer)—attention to physical rehabilitation goes hand in hand with emotional rehabilitation. One could fall into total helplessness when confronted with injuries and disease or one can choose to be as alive as the body permits. Working through the early aspects of emotional healing—tears, self-care, support system, medication—through the stitches of reality and legitimacy of being angry for having to deal with debilities can provide the grounding for investing in the physical rehab, for investing in the surgeries, for investing in the medications aimed at providing quality of life, for investing in the physical therapy often necessary, for investing in the training for living without certain abilities. In turn investing physical and psychic energy into the sometimes-torturous programs can be part of the emotional healing: "I am meeting the challenges, I am alive, I am moving on."

Hospitals and various agencies provide a myriad of resources for physical rehabilitation for physical problems, and they often provide support groups for people marching or dragging themselves through the process. It really doesn't matter if you march or drag. It's getting into it and sticking with it that counts; it's giving up the "I can do it all myself"; it's giving up the "Why bother, I'll sit here and suffer" attitude often based on anger but anger turned inward and then taken out on caretakers in sneaky or not-so-sneaky, demanding ways.

The resources are there. Just look in the Yellow Pages. To get into rehabilitation takes guts, the strength developed by starting with the gentler aspects of healing—the tears, the ointments, etc.—and moving into the harsh but necessary realities referred to as stitches.

Rehabilitation may start with the activities and perspectives suggested in earlier parts of this book. It will continue as a lifelong process, but notice the word "life" is involved—not merely existing. Major wounds, especially, may need a lifetime of intermittent treatment—more washings, more ointments, more medications, more bandages, more stitches, and perhaps newer versions of rehabilitation. This need over time for attention to the wound is what I am referring to in the next chapter.

Chapter 7 Exercises

1. You may well already be into this part of healing via work you're doing in regard to the material in earlier chapters—especially in the chapter "Medication." Now may be the time to start a new journal or a separate one titled "The Future" and to begin to make plans for investing in your life and your future.

2. Or you may want to use the following chart or create one based on it that fits you better:

AREA	GOAL/ CHANGE/ ACTIVITY	INITIAL ACTION POSSIBLE TOWARD THAT GOAL	FUTURE STEPS, ACTIONS TOWARD THAT GOAL
Physical			
Educational			
Creative			
Home			

Work			
Friendships/ Relationships/ Family			
Spiritual			
Other:			
Other:			

3. Either from a journal or from a list or from column 3 in the chart, decide on one small thing you can do to show yourself that you are getting active in your rehabilitation program.

4. If your list or chart has many items on it, it may feel overwhelming and actually get in the way of getting anything done. You may want to go through your list (column 2, if you used the chart) and prioritize the items you listed, i.e., if there are forty items on the list, assign each a number from your highest priority (#1) to your lowest (#40). Proceed to set tangible goals that show you are working on your higher priorities first; later the lower ones may change in their status when you redo the prioritizing. It is useful to redo your priority list periodically because priorities are not carved in stone. If you find yourself not getting something done, ask yourself if its priority has lessened. Use the priority list also for setting standards: higher standards for the higher items, lower standards for the lower items.

5. Be careful not to allow the goals to become "shoulds." Remember "shoulds" get sabotaged. Listen to how you talk to yourself. Catch the sneaky "should"—"It will be good for me!" "I have to do this"—and revise them into forms of "want"—"I want to do this because it will help me feel more alive," "I am going to do this because when I'm finished I will know I've met a challenge, and that will help me feel better."

CHAPTER 8

SCAR TISSUE

With most injuries or wounds there are scars, and with emotional injuries there are usually scars as well. As I mentioned at the end of chapter 7, "Rehabilitation," some wounds may call for a lifetime of intermittent treatment and rehabilitation.

When the emotional wound is related to a physical problem—loss of a limb, loss of sight, illness that causes drastic limitations in one way or another, disfiguring injuries—we have the physical reminder of the wounding that can trigger the pangs of the emotional wound at odd moments; and it is at those odd moments that we feel the scars and need to attend to them and recycle through some or all of the healing steps. (I have emphysema, and with the use of an inhaler twice a day, I can function quite normally. Friends forget I have a serious disease; I often forget my problem myself. Yet when I try to walk uphill with a friend, I cannot keep pace. I apologize. Inside I am pissed. Pissed at my youthful stupidity of smoking; pissed at now paying the price. I have to stop and forgive myself and internally apologize to myself. Sometimes in the North Carolina mountains when I have to forgo a path I once easily climbed, tears come; I talk gently to myself, the kindness of my companion supports me, and I accept what I cannot do and find paths I can climb. It also reminds me to do the breathing exercises I was taught and not to forget to use my inhaler.)

Scar tissue consists of the reminders that create the flashback of the original loss, of the original wound. With emotional wounds, the scars are often invisible, but they are still there and need attention. As with physical disabilities and the accompanying emotional scarring, invisible scars from the death of a loved one or of a relationship or of any other major life change (e.g., rape) need attention and recycling through various aspects of healing. Reminders can pop out of nowhere. Something we see—a song, a book title, a scene in a movie, frightening news—can bring the painful feelings rushing back. (When I've been sitting on a plane and saw a grey rim of hair on a bald head, I have had tears well up as I reexperience a twinge of the pain of no longer having my dead poppa there for me. Now, when that happens, because he died over twenty years ago, I can move on merely by thinking of pleasant times with him, smile and feel some form of his presence.) "Reminders" may come in the form of another death or loss. People often wonder why they are so upset when their pet dies. First it may be a terrible loss, a loss of a faithful companion; but sometimes it may simply be it touches that place within, those scars from previous deaths that need more attention. If you had to get too quickly back into "taking care of things" when a loved one died, you may find yourself needing to return to that death when you are faced with the death of a work colleague.

If you didn't take the time to reclaim yourself after the death of a relationship, small annoyances, similar to those of the past, in a new relationship may explode into giant issues; again, the issues from the old relationship need to be dealt with for what they are—issues from a dead relationship that serve to keep it partially alive and interfering with your present relationship. As suggested earlier in this book, working with a therapist to finish up unfinished business can be of great help.

Because the scars are invisible, others often do not understand when we feel the recurring pain. It is especially important to have some people in our support system who understand and who do not need for us to pretend we are totally OK.

With invisible scars, it also is especially important that we, ourselves, do not ignore our own pain when it recurs and that we allow ourselves to engage in some of the healing activities whether it be crying, being kind to oneself, using a ritual, talking with a friend, and/or refocusing some rehabilitation activities. Others may not know what to do that will be helpful; sometimes we simply need to tell them, "Please just be here."

Anniversaries of deaths, losses, and life changes are a special form of event that needs attention. It is on anniversaries that we often have waves of the original grief pour over us in the forms of irritability, "unexplained" sadness, even aches and physical pains. Since anniversaries are something we can keep track of, it is a good idea to mark your calendar and to plan to be especially kind to yourself on that day and even a few days before and after. (On the first anniversary of my poppa's death, I took three days off—the day he died and the days before and after.) Anniversaries are dates on which you need to allow for few demands or activities that call for concerted energy.

Sometimes it helps to plan some rituals for the anniversaries. One might visit the grave on the anniversary and allow the tears to fall. One might return to journaling and/or ask a friend to be with you that day. One might engage in a ritual that celebrates the dead individual's life and contributions to your life. (In the Catholic tradition, saints' "feast days" are the days they died, not their birthdays. My poppa died on December 7. I declared that day his "feast day," and I engage in activities that are a celebration of his life and of his kindnesses toward me.)

It doesn't help to ignore the scars. When the reminders occur, when the anniversaries arrive, allow the tears to flow if you find they are settling "behind your eyes." Apply the ointments that work to soothe you. Wrap yourself in the bandage of people who can be there for you. Use the medications that help you feel alive. Acknowledge the realities. Reinvest in your rehabilitation program.

Chapter 8 Exercises

1. List the losses you've experienced (deaths of loved ones, of friends, of colleagues, of pets; injuries; debilitating illnesses; traumatic events that caused losses and/or life changes). First just list them—don't worry about dates or accuracy of details; then list them in order of the painfulness for you—just go by your gut—#1= most painful, through as many as you listed.

LOSSES	PAINFULNESS OF THE LOSSES

2. Once you have identified the losses you are aware of and identified the seriousness and painfulness of each of them for you, start with the most painful (probably the most current one, but not always) and see if you can identify some of the events and occurrences that touch the scar tissue and need attention; this could include anniversary dates, visits to a physician, running into someone who looks like the dead loved one, etc. In column 3, write ideas for self-talk, self-care, rituals, etc., that might help when that scar tissue aches. Get supportive friends, family members, or therapists to help with suggestions.

LOSS #1 IN TERMS OF PAINFULNESS	EVENTS/OCCURRENCES THAT SET OFF THE SCAR TISSUE	THINGS I CAN DO TO ATTEND TO THE PAIN THAT COMES WITH THOSE EVENTS/ OCCURRENCES

3. Create charts such as the one above for each of your major losses. Add to columns 2 and 3 in each of your charts as you discover what starts the scar tissue hurting and as you try out "ointments," "bandages," "medications," "stitches," and/or "rehab" and find ones that work for you.

4. Contract to be alert to items in column 2 and to do at least one thing from column 3 when you notice the presence of cues for pain.

CHAPTER 9

CONCLUSION

In the introductory chapter, I recommended that you glean from this book what fits for you. I suggested that you take the ideas and suggestions as just that, suggestions. Yes, I am an "expert" on grieving, but you are the expert on your grieving.

What you decide to implement from the chapters in this book is your "treatment plan." In general gathering strategies from each of the chapters can be helpful. Remember, it is not a matter of "I should do these things," but rather, "I want to do these things because I selected them as things that will help me heal and recover from the loss or losses I've suffered."

Are you allowing yourself the tears that may be right on the surface or perhaps deep inside the well of your feelings? Are you choking them back, or are you finding times and places to let them flow? Are you less apologetic about them and accept them as a normal part of healing?

Have you set up an array of ointments, those activities and investments of self that are soothing and represent self-care? Among these, hopefully, are physical self-care (nutrition, exercise, etc.) and emotional self-care (journaling, meditation, prayer, laughter, etc.).

Have you identified those people in your life space whether geographically near or far who can be counted as parts of your bandage, of your support system? Are you identifying and using the various forms your support system takes: emotional support, emotional stretching, social validation? Are you making sure not to expect or to ask only one other person to be your bandage?

Have you stocked your emotional medicine chest with healthy activities that serve as distractions, that may serve to provide a sense of control, that may be reminders of life going on? Are you working, playing, laughing, taking care of business?

Are you acknowledging the realities—dead, over, finished, gone, change? Are you accepting any angry feelings you may have? Are you, at least, accepting that facing reality is a part of the healing, if not this moment, as soon as is possible for you? Are you finding healthy, nondestructive (of yourself and/or others) ways of expressing your anger or other feelings some people designate as unsuitable, bad, negative—expressing them so as to clear them away and make room for once again experiencing delight, joy, happiness, and other "good" feelings?

Are you starting to make plans for the future? Are you engaging in forms of rehabilitation that are appropriate for your situation, your loss? Are you, at least, aware that rehabilitation is important to engage in and that once you've done more of the early healing work, it does constitute the beginning of truly moving on?

Even if you've moved on, scars remain and need attention. Noting anniversaries and devising ways to honor the dead loved one or to honor yourself if it is an anniversary of a traumatic event for you are ways of attending to the scars. Have you begun to make some plans for handling the reminders, the cues for pain that often come when you least expect?

Healing is a process, and the deeper and more extensive the wound, the more important it is to engage in the full process.

A small wound may need only an ouch and a medicated Band-Aid. Then again, a small wound may bring memories of or fears about old, deeper wounds. Attending to them is a major aspect of healing—not ignoring them but examining the wound and seeing what it is all about and then determining what forms the treatment needs to take are important responses.

This has been a general book about the practicalities of healing from losses, of healing the emotional wounds that come from deaths, from dreams killed, from disabilities, from illnesses. In the appendix, I will list books, with a brief description of their content, that contain specific information and ideas that have been useful to me and/or to my clients.

Whatever you take from this book is your choice. No one else can write your healing plan for you. You can take what I've offered as a guideline. You can take what has been presented and seek a professional (counselor, therapist, clergy member) to help you develop a plan that is right for you. You can throw the whole thing away and decide it's not useful, but I would challenge that. If your temptation is to toss this book on a shelf—or out the window—check it out one more time and see if there aren't at least a few things that might help you feel better in terms of cleansing, anointing, bandaging, medicating, and stitching. Sometimes if the loss and the wound feel so immense and the healing process seems too overwhelming, the first step may be to seek professional help and then, with that person as a support and guide, move toward a point when you are able to engage in the healing process. I especially recommend seeking professional help over trying to cope via overuse of medications, real ones or "-isms"—alcoholism, workaholism, etc.

Whatever you decide to do constitutes your personal **Treatment Plan.**

Chapter 9 Exercises

If you decided to persist with using this book as a guide, here is where you might want to consolidate your "treatment plan."

My "Treatment Plan"

For each of the headings that follow, fill in what you think fits for you. Going back and looking at your responses to the various exercises might help. If you skipped the exercises, this may be the time to do them. If you do not want to do them, fine; cull from your recollection of what you read in the chapters' ideas, suggestions, activities, etc., that would feel appropriate for you under each heading. It might also help to have a friend or a professional person assist you.

Once you have filled in the spaces below as much as you can or want to, it can be helpful to focus on a few—perhaps one or two from each category, especially the first five categories to begin with. (I've actually put my "treatment plan" on the refrigerator and added to it as needed; I also put a list of the major people who constitute my bandage plus their phone numbers on a sheet of paper on the bulletin board beside my kitchen phone.)

When we are in the midst of depression and the pain, it is hard to come up with what might help; making lists and having them readily available (sort of a Chinese menu) can help at those times when the pain hits and we don't know what to do.

Washing the Wound (Tears)

Applying Ointment (Self-Care)

Bandaging (Support Systems)

Medication (Activities, Distraction, Work, Etc.)

Stitches (Realities, "Unacceptable" Feelings)

Rehabilitation (Getting on with Life)

Scar Tissue (Plans for Anniversaries, Etc.)

RECOMMENDED REFERENCES

Death

Kübler-Ross, E. 1969. *On Death and Dying: What the Dying Have to Teach Doctors, Nurses, Clergy and Their Own Families.* New York: Macmillan Publishing Co., Inc.

The first book for everyday people on the topic of death by the expert Elizabeth Kübler-Ross. Her work serves as the basis for much of the writing and research on death and dying during the following decades to the present.

Kübler-Ross, E. 1974. *Questions and Answers on Death and Dying.* New York: Macmillan Publishing Co., Inc.

A practical follow-up book to Kübler-Ross's classic book, listed above.

Grollman, E. A., ed. 1981. *What Helped Me When My Loved One Died.* Boston: Beacon Press.

This book deals with specific losses: what helps when a child dies (includes stillbirths, accidents, and illnesses to loss of adult children), when a spouse dies (includes "normal" deaths and suicide), when a parent dies, and even when a classmate, parishioner, or patient dies.

The Grollmans have published many books on the topic of death and loss for adults and for children, all of them possibly of great help. I've included one other further in this listing.

O'Connor, N. 1984. *Letting Go with Love: The Grieving Process.* Apache Junction, AZ: La Mariposa Press.

Kübler-Ross gave her endorsement to this book, which builds on Kübler-Ross's stages and moves on through dealing with different types of deaths: spouse, parent, child, friends and siblings, and death by suicide.

Staudacher, Carol. 1987. *Beyond Grief: A Guide for Recovering from the Death of a Loved One*. Oakland, CA: New Harbinger Publications, Inc.

In addition to a very useful treatment of the experience of grief, including the need for ritual and dealing with anger and with guilt, Staudacher also offers useful suggestions and ideas in regard to specific losses: spouse, parent, child, childhood losses, accidental deaths, suicides, and murders. She also offers useful materials for helping those who are grieving and guidelines for support groups.

General Losses: Death, Divorce, and Other Losses

James, J. W., and R. Friedman. 1998. *The Grief Recovery Handbook: The Action Program for Moving beyond Death, Divorce, and Other Losses*. Rev. ed. New York: HarperCollins.

James and Friedman provide some useful ideas and strategies for moving through the grief process whether it be related to a death, a major health change, financial changes, and other changes, including "positive changes." They also are helpful with discussions and suggestions of how to deal with others' reactions.

Deits, B. 1992. *Life After Loss: A Personal Guide Dealing with Death, Divorce, Job Change, and Relocation*. Tulsa, AZ: Fisher Books.

Deits covers many practical aspects of coping with loss and growing from the loss experience.

End of a Relationship

Fisher, B. 1981, 1994. *Rebuilding: When Your Relationship Ends*. 4th printing. San Luis Obispo, CA: Impact Publishers.

This book has become somewhat of a classic in terms of helping people deal with the end of a relationship and moving on. It is endorsed by Virginia Satir. It applies Kübler-Ross's stages of grief and then goes on to ideas and suggestions for moving toward a new and healthy relationship.

Colegrove, M., H. H. Bloomfield, and P. McWilliams. 1991. *How to Survive the Loss of a Love*. Los Angeles: Prelude Press.

This little book is the work of a consultant, a psychologist, and a poet. With a basis of sound psychological principles, it takes the reader through the many emotions and setbacks involved in the ending of a love relationship. It is a book to be experienced, not simply read.

Miscarriages, Stillborns, and Infant's Death

Ilse, S. 1982. *Empty Arms: Coping with Miscarriage, Stillbirth and Infant Death*. Maple Plain, MN: Wintergreen Press.

Despite the frequency of miscarriages, the topics of miscarriage and stillbirth are often overlooked, and this book provides useful ideas and discussions on both. Ilse also deals with abortion, SIDS, and other pre- and postnatal losses.

Trauma

Matsakis, A. 1992. *I Can't Get Over It: A Handbook for Trauma Survivors*. Oakland, CA: New Harbinger Publications, Inc.

This is an extremely useful book for a variety of survivors of trauma. Matsakis first deals with the general aspects of reactions to trauma and the process of healing from trauma. She then looks in detail at traumatic reactions and healing from specific forms of traumas including crimes committed by strangers, rape and sexual assault, domestic violence and sexual abuse, natural catastrophes, vehicular accidents, and war and combat.

Rape

Johnson, K. M. 1985. *If You Are Raped: What Every Woman Needs to Know*. Holmes Beach, FL: Learning Publications, Inc.

This is a very practical book focusing on "taking care of business" in relationship to the healing from rape. It does touch the emotional aspects, but mainly it deals with healing in terms of taking action, although it does not support forcing a victim to take action.

McEvoy, A. W., and J. B. Brookings. 1984. *If She Is Raped: A Book for Husbands, Fathers and Male Friends.* Holmes Beach, FL: Learning Publications, Inc.

Men in the lives of female rape victims often have their own grief issues and feelings of guilt. This book addresses those feelings and offers suggestions on what can be helpful and what is not helpful to the victim.

Specific Populations

Women

Silverman, P. R. 1981. *Helping Women Cope with Grief.* Beverly Hills: Sage Publications.

Silverman first provides some useful general thoughts on grief and grieving and then focuses on three specific losses experienced by many women: widowhood, losses as a birthmother, and battering.

Adolescents, Teens, Young Adults

Gootman, M. E. 1994. *When a Friend Dies: A Book for Teens about Grieving and Healing.* Minneapolis, MN: Free Spirit Publishing, Inc.

This small book provides a beautiful, personalized, nonacademic approach to coping with the death of a friend.

Grollman, E. A. 1993. *Straight Talk about Death for Teenagers: How to Cope with Losing Someone You Love.* Boston: Beacon Press.

Grollman speaks gently yet directly to teens and young adults who have experienced the death of a loved one, explaining the feelings often experienced, providing advice for special relationships and circumstances and personal survival strategies.

Rituals

Imber-Black, E., and J. Roberts. 1992. *Rituals for Our Times: Celebrating, Healing, and Changing Our Lives and Our Relationships.* New York: HarperCollins Publishers.

Imber-Black and Roberts provide both an overview of the importance of rituals in our lives and specific suggestions for rituals that can be helpful in a number of different situations.

Beck, R., and S. B. Metrick. 1990. *The Art of Ritual: A Guide to Creating and Performing Your Own Rituals for Growth and Change.* Berkeley, CA: Celestial Arts.
Another useful book for help with developing individualized rituals.

Support Systems

Pines, A. M., and E. Aronson. 1981. *Burnout: From Tedium to Personal Growth.* New York: Free Press.
One of the first books looking at burnout. Chapter 7 is especially useful in regard to delineating support systems.

Self-Care

Bensen, R. 2000. *The Relaxation Response.* With M. Klipper. New York: HarperTorch.
This is an update and expansion of the classic 1975 publication. The benefits of the practice of systematic relaxation are presented with research backing, and methods of using and applying systematic relation are provided. This is a must for anyone trying to deal with the stress of grief.

Davis, M., E. R. Eshelman, and M. McKay. 1995. *The Relaxation and Stress Reduction Workbook.* 4th ed. Oakland, CA: New Harbinger Publications, Inc.
This is one of best sources for the many techniques available to deal with stress, including meditation, breathing, thought stopping, refuting irrational ideas, and even nutritional suggestions.

Get Published, Inc!
Thorofare, NJ 08086
13 April, 2010
BA2010103